VOL. I
IMAGINATION

PERSONAL ILLUMINATIONS

MY CREATIVE JOURNAL

JAMES C. CHRISTENSEN

PERSONAL ILLUMINATIONS

VOL. I
IMAGINATION

SHADOW
MOUNTAIN

FOR ALEX DARAIS, J. ROMAN ANDEUS, FRANZ JOHANSEN AND FRANK MAGLEBY WHO GOT ME STARTED

ACKNOWLEDGEMENTS

The author and the publisher have made every effort to secure proper copyright information. Any inadvertent error will be corrected in subsequent printings. Mr. Christensen's notes on the book *How to Think Like Leonardo da Vinci: Seven Steps to Genius Every Day*, were from a lecture he attended. The book is by Michael J. Gelb, copyright © 1998 by Michael J. Gelb. Used by permission of Dell Publishing, a division of Random House, Inc.

© 2000 The Greenwich Workshop, Inc. and James C. Christensen

ISBN 1-57345-855-4

Designed by Peter Landa and Milly Iacono
Printed in the United States of America

10   9   8   7   6   5   4   3   2   1

INTRODUCTION

J A M E S   C.   C H R I S T E N S E N

I had a conversation recently with a woman at a gallery that was showing my paintings and sculpture. It was typical of many conversations with people who have seen my work. "You are so lucky to have been blessed with an imagination," she said. "I have no imagination at all. I can't think up anything!" This was followed by the question I am most frequently asked: "Where do you get your ideas?"

These comments, repeated often as I talk with folks about my work, set me thinking. Where do I get my ideas? How does one "think up" things? Where does inspiration come from? I have never had a problem thinking up things and have had a very active imagination since childhood. But how does it work?

It seems that many adults see imagination and creativity as something reserved for artists, writers, and other "creative" types. But I don't agree with that. I believe that everyone has an imagination, everyone has the potential to be creative. I think that the process comes more easily to some people than to others, but with practice we all have access to imagination and creative problem solving, no matter where our interests and talents lie.

This book is an introduction to creating a journal of imagination. I think the best place to start exercising your imagination is by paying attention and making note of the world around you (and the world within you). I keep a sketchbook to record ideas, to remember connections between ideas, and to just let imagination happen. (The drawings in this book are from my sketchbooks.) Not everybody draws, or thinks they can draw, and you might be more comfortable writing down ideas and observations. That's fine! Sometimes I even paste things into my journals. Do whatever works for you, but be brave and push yourself a little. What's the worst that can happen? You turn the page and start over!

James Christensen

THIS BOOK IS MEANT TO BE WRITTEN IN.
A NEW JOURNAL OR SKETCHBOOK IS A
BEAUTIFUL, PRISTINE THING, AND MAKING
THE FIRST MARK IN IT IS ALWAYS DIFFICULT.

ESPECIALLY IF YOU THINK THAT FIRST THING
HAS TO BE REALLY, REALLY GOOD. SO I'M
GOING TO HELP YOU GET OVER THAT IMAGI-
NARY STUMBLING BLOCK.

WRITE HERE OR...

ꓷOOꓷLE HERE OR...

SCRIBBLE HERE OR...

DRAW HERE OR...

YOU MUST MAKE SOME MARK IN THIS BOX
BEFORE YOU TURN THE PAGE. DRAW, WRITE,
SCRIBBLE, PASTE... DO SOMETHING AND THEN
YOU'LL BE ON YOUR WAY TO FILLING IN YOUR
VERY OWN JOURNAL OF THE IMAGINATION.

IMAGINATION WORKS LIKE A CARD FILE. ROWS AND ROWS OF LITTLE DRAWERS FILLED WITH THOUSANDS AND THOUSANDS OF LITTLE CARDS~THAT IS WHAT OUR MIND IS LIKE. EACH OF US HAS UNIQUE EXPERIENCES WHICH MAKE UNIQUE SETS OF CARDS.

WHEN WE'RE BORN, THE CARDS ARE MOSTLY EMPTY, BUT EVERYTHING IN OUR LIVES FILLS THE CARDS.

THE BIGGER OUR CARD CATALOGUE IS, THE MORE POTENTIAL FOR IMAGINATIVE THINKING WE HAVE.

AQUARIUM

MARIONETTE

LOUDSPEAKER

PIRATE

POMPOSITY

LION

REVELATIONS

YOUR GREAT (OR
EVEN MEDIOCRE)
REVELATIONS AND
INSIGHTS GO HERE....

INSIGHTS

...AS WELL
AS HERE

YOU START HERE:

TROLL

DIGNITARY

PIGLET

PLEASE FILL!!

HEY, YOU JUST MADE SOME CARDS!

How do you fill up your cards? With people, thoughts, memories,

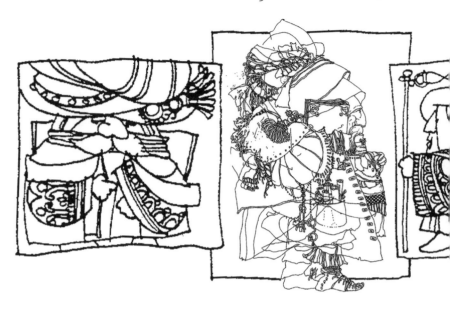

IMAGINATION, OBSERVATION...OR THROUGH YOUR SIX SENSES.

We can fill our cards through all our six senses. Try writing or drawing your sensory input here:

SEE

TOUCH

HEAR

SMELL

TASTE

INSPIRATION

YES, THERE IS A SIXTH SENSE!
INSPIRATION ~ OR INTUITION IF
YOU PREFER ~ IS AN IMPORTANT
SOURCE OF NEW IDEAS.
DON'T IGNORE IT!

MORE OF YOUR INPUT:

WRITE, DOODLE, SKETCH, PAINT, DRAW,
SCRIBBLE, SCRATCH, MARK, OR PASTE.

YOU DON'T HAVE TO STAY IN THE LINES!

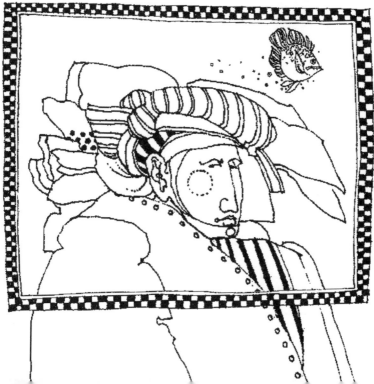

So what is imagination? How does it work? Imagination is combining your cards in new and unique ways.

MARIONETTE · BANJO · LETTER
CANDLE · DIVING BOARD
FURRY · PUDDING
MERMAID · ROWBOAT · ANGE
AVIATOR · AQUARIUM
SPACESHIP
GOBLINS · GNOMES
SPRITES

PLATYPUS

CURMUDGEON

ARMADILLO

MACHINERY

IMPOSTOR

RADARSCOPE

TURKEY

GYPSY

EGGPLANT

CROW

ACROBAT

MANATEE

MINOTAUR

HERMIT

MARMOT

MANCHURIA

STILTS

TYPHOON

GADGET

ELEPHANT

FLAMBOYANT

BIRDS-OF-A-FEATHER

PROBOSCIS

MERMAID

AVIATOR

NOW IT'S TIME TO MAKE SOME STRANGE CARD CATALOGUE CONNECTIONS AND UNIQUE LEAPS OF LOGIC.

MERMAID AVIATOR

NO COMBINATIONS ARE TOO FAR-FETCHED OR RIDICULOUS. SOMETIMES THE BEST THING ABOUT AN IDEA IS THAT IT LEADS TO A BETTER ONE.

YOU CAN MAKE COMBINATIONS
USING WORDS, TOO.

| ZIPPER | + | LOCK | = | ZIPLOC BAG |

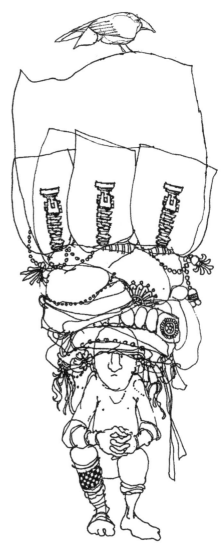

ILIKE COSTUMES AND ARMOR, SO I PAY SPECIAL ATTENTION TO OLD ART ENGRAVINGS, COSTUMES AND DESIGN BOOKS, AND I VISIT ANY MUSEUM WITH AN ARMOR COLLECTION. I DRAW COSTUMES AND ARMOR IN MY JOURNAL.

I'M ALSO INTERESTED IN BUGS.

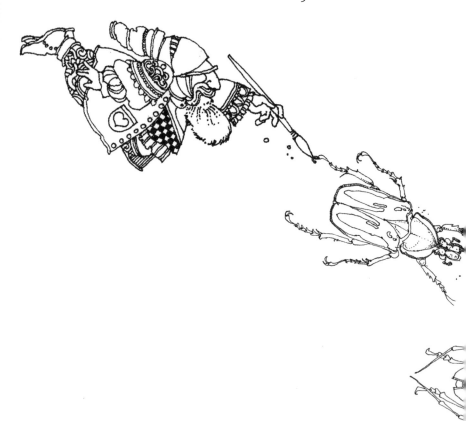

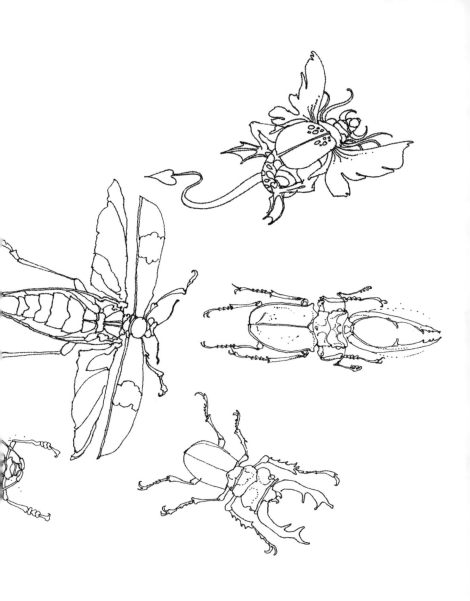

YOU CAN DO IT VISUALLY...OR IN WORDS.

WHEN I LEAST EXPECT IT, A DRAWING COMES OUT THAT COMBINES THE CARDS IN UNEXPECTED WAYS.

CAUTION:

AS WE GET OLDER, WE GET INTO THINKING-RUTS OR LEARNED PATTERNS OF THOUGHT.

SOME THINKING-RUTS ARE GOOD.

- STOP AT RED LIGHTS.
- DUCK WHEN YOU GO THROUGH LOW DOORWAYS.

IDENTIFY YOUR RUTS.

ASK YOURSELF: IS THIS THE **BEST** WAY TO DO IT OR IS IT JUST THE WAY I AM **USED** TO DOING IT, OR THE WAY I WAS **TAUGHT** TO DO IT?

GETTING OUT OF THE RUTS:
- PICK A COLOR AND NOTICE IT ALL DAY.
- DRIVE HOME A DIFFERENT WAY.
- TRY EATING SOMETHING NEW.
- TAKE A TRIP TO A TOWN NEAR YOU THAT YOU'VE NEVER VISITED. EXPLORE IT.
- STAY OFF THE HIGHWAY FOR A DAY.

SOME IDEAS:

DIFFERENT ISN'T ALWAYS BETTER.
BUT THE SAME IS NEVER BETTER.

THE ARTS OFFER US LIMITLESS NEW CARDS FOR OUR FILES AND STIMULATE US TO MAKE NEW COMBINATIONS.

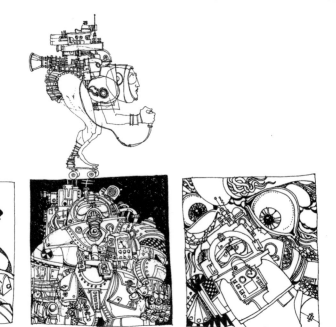

"WHAT IF ARTISTS ARE NOT AT THE PERIPHERY OF A TECHNOLOGICAL SOCIETY, BUT AT ITS CORE? ART IS NOT THE DECORATION AROUND TECHNOLOGY, BUT IS THE SOURCE."   ~ROLLO MAY

WITH A LITTLE EFFORT, YOU WILL FIND YOUR OWN MEANING IN ART THAT IS VALID FOR YOU, AND MUCH MORE IMPORTANT FOR YOUR LIFE THAN SOMEONE ELSE'S MEANING.

WHAT IS THE MONA LISA SMILING ABOUT?

SONGS FROM MY TEENS, AND MEMORIES CONNECTED TO THEM:

LET'S PRACTICE:
LET'S PUSH THE ENVELOPE.

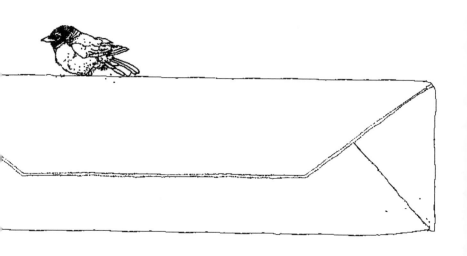

PRACTICE, PRACTICE, PRACTICE.

MAKE UP A STORY ABOUT THIS PICTURE.
YOU CAN ADD DRAWINGS, TOO.

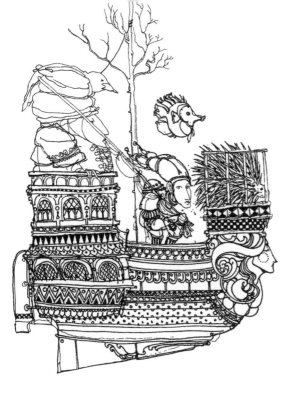

S EEING HAPPENS WITH YOUR EYES, BUT
OBSERVING MIGHT TAKE TWO OR THREE
OR ALL OF YOUR SENSES.

WHAT DO I KNOW ABOUT MY FAVORITE RELATIVE? WHAT SHOULD I KNOW? PEOPLE ARE GREAT RESOURCES, TOO.

DON'T FORGET THE BOXES PEOPLE COME IN! LOOK AT ARCHITECTURE, TOO.

TRY SOMETHING NEW TODAY.

BUY OPERA TICKETS.
TAKE A BOAT RIDE.
HAVE LUNCH AT A
  MONGOLIAN RESTAURANT.
TAKE YOUR BIRD
  FOR A WALK.
TAKE UP BADMINTON.
TAKE TUBA LESSONS.

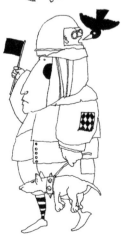

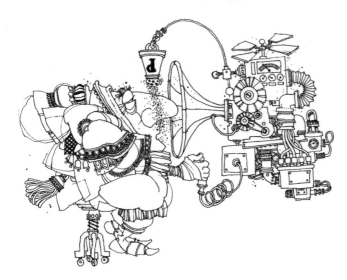

HARNESS YOUR SNEEZE POWER.

FIRSTHAND EXPERIENCES ARE THE STRONGEST AND MOST IMMEDIATE, BUT HEARING, SEEING, OR READING A GOOD STORY CAN CHANGE ONE'S LIFE.

MOVIES   MUSIC   STORIES

BOOKS   RADIO   PLAYS

"IT IS INDISPUTABLY EVIDENT THAT A GREAT PART OF EVERY MAN'S LIFE MUST BE EMPLOYED IN COLLECTING MATERIALS FOR THE EXERCISE OF GENIUS. INVENTION, STRICTLY SPEAKING, IS LITTLE MORE THAN A NEW COMBINATION OF THOSE IMAGES WHICH HAVE BEEN PREVIOUSLY GATHERED AND DEPOSITED IN THE MEMORY: NOTHING CAN COME OF NOTHING. HE WHO HAS LAID UP NO MATERIALS CAN PRODUCE NO COMBINATIONS." ~SIR JOSHUA REYNOLDS, 18TH CENTURY PAINTER

GATHER AND DEPOSIT MATERIALS HERE.

Y OU HAVE A UNIQUE SET OF FILE CARDS,
FILLED OUT OVER A LIFETIME. WE WILL
ALL HAVE SOME CARDS IN COMMON, BUT
YOUR EXPERIENCES CREATE A SET DIFFER-
ENT THAN ANYONE ELSE'S.

THIS IS
UNIQUELY ME

This is
uniquely me.

This is
uniquely me.

THIS IS UNIQUELY
ME

To Train Your Mind to Think Creatively:

- Document your experience.
- Have your journal or sketchbook with you so you can write or doodle when the opportunity allows.
- Make notes to trigger your memory and capture thoughts and impressions.
- Draw pictures, or stick photographs or maps of places you went or want to visit, into your journal.

TAKE A WALK, YOU'RE DONE FOR TODAY.

NOW YOU'VE GOT ALL THE TOOLS TO BE CREATIVE. THE REST OF THIS BOOK IS ALL YOURS TO EXERCISE YOUR IMAGINATION.

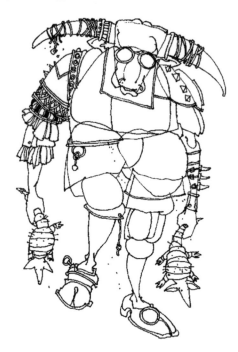

"THE WHOLE OF THE VISIBLE UNIVERSE IS
ONLY A STOREHOUSE OF IMAGES AND
SIGNS TO WHICH THE IMAGINATION ASSIGNS
A PLACE AND RELATIVE VALUE: IT IS A KIND
OF NOURISHMENT THAT THE IMAGINATION
MUST DIGEST AND TRANSFORM."

~ BAUDELAIRE

TAKE TIME TO
MAKE NOTES ON
WHAT YOU'RE
EXPERIENCING
AND HOW YOU'RE
FEELING.

Love is a word that has been taken out of modern criticism. But it is the center of what life is about.

I love this food.

I love this smell.

I LOVE THE WAY THIS FEELS.

I LOVE THIS SOUND.

I LOVE THIS COLOR.

If you find yourself fishing out of the same bucket for ideas, it's time to make a bigger bucket!

WHAT'S IN YOUR BUCKET OF IDEAS?

EXERCISE YOUR "WHAT IF" MUSCLE.
WHAT IF THE WORLD REALLY WAS FLAT?
WHAT IF PIGS COULD FLY? WHAT
IF PEOPLE LAID EGGS?

TAKE AN IDEA AND RUN WITH IT AS
FAR AS IT WILL GO.

"As one grows older, one sees the impossibility of imposing your will on the chaos with brute force. But if you are patient, there may come that moment when, while eating an apple, the solution presents itself politely and says: here I am." ~ Albert Einstein

LET A DILEMMA SIMMER. YOUR MIND
WORKS ON THINGS EVEN WHEN YOU'RE NOT
PAYING ATTENTION.

SOMETIMES THE BEST CONNECTIONS ARE MADE WHILE WE MEANDER, DAYDREAM, OR CONTEMPLATE THE THINGS AROUND US.

GREAT IDEAS I GOT IN THE SHOWER, WALKING THE DOG, OR DOZING BEFORE THE ALARM WENT OFF... AGAIN.

IF LIFE IS A JOURNEY, WHAT
KIND OF BOAT AM I IN?

ONE HUNDRED AND ONE THINGS TO DO WITH AN ALLIGATOR:

1. SHOES
2. HANDBAGS
3. GO FOR A WALK ON A LEASH
4. TOOTH NECKLACE
5. STEW
6. WRESTLE
7. GO TO THE BEACH
8. GO SEE "CROCODILE DUNDEE"
9. SHARE A GATORADE
10. SQUARE DANCE

THE FIRST TEN ARE EASY, BUT THE REST WILL EXERCISE YOUR IMAGINATION.

11. BUGGY RACES (SWAMP, THAT IS!)
12. LISTEN TO ROCK AND ROLL MUSIC
13. RIDE ON A ROLLER COASTER
14.
15.
16.
17.
18.
19.
20.
21.
22.
23.

PUSH AN IDEA FURTHER THAN YOU EVER
THOUGHT YOU COULD.

NOTHING NEW UNDER THE SUN

"ORIGINALITY IS THE ART OF CONCEALING
ONE'S SOURCES."   ~WHO SAID THIS?

SOME FAVORITE IDEAS THAT I'VE HEARD AND NOW OWN:

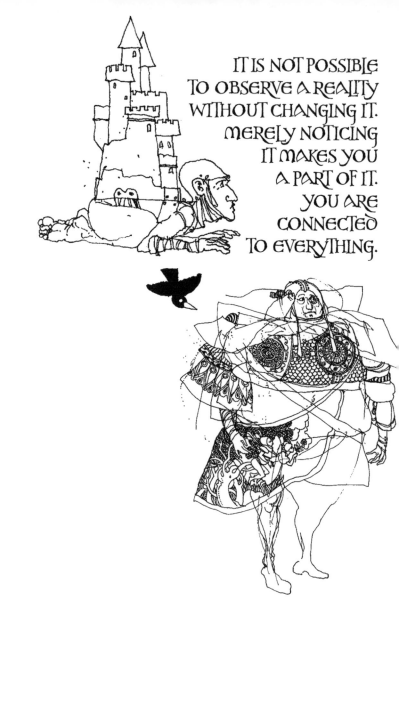

IT IS NOT POSSIBLE
TO OBSERVE A REALITY
WITHOUT CHANGING IT.
MERELY NOTICING
IT MAKES YOU
A PART OF IT.
YOU ARE
CONNECTED
TO EVERYTHING.

THERE IS NO SUCH THING AS OBJECTIVITY~
TAKING THE POINT OF VIEW THAT WE WILL
HAVE NO POINT OF VIEW IS A POINT OF VIEW.

HOW TO THINK LIKE LEONARDO DA VINCI

SEVEN STEPS TO EVERYDAY GENIUS:

1. BE CURIOUS
2. THINK FOR YOURSELF (YOU ARE AN AGENT)
3. SHARPEN YOUR SENSES
4. EMBRACE AMBIGUITY
5. MAKE CONNECTIONS
6. BALANCE ART AND SCIENCE, LOGIC AND IMAGINATION, WITH INTUITION
7. BALANCE BODY AND MIND

THE END (BUT IT'S NOT OVER, YET).
GO BACK AND FILL IN THE BLANKS.
WHEN YOU FINISH, YOU WILL HAVE CREATED
YOUR OWN IDEA BOOK. IT'S A MAP OF YOUR
IMAGINATION. KEEP IT. GUARD IT CAREFULLY.
AS LONG AS YOU LIVE (AND MAYBE BEYOND),
YOU ARE ADDING CARDS TO YOUR FILE.
AND NOW THAT YOU HAVE AN IDEA BOOK,
YOU'LL NEVER BE BORED AGAIN.
START ANOTHER ONE!